D1518067

Yellow Umbrella Books are published by Capstone Press
151 Good Counsel Drive, P.O. Box 669, Mankato, Minnesota 56002
www.capstonepress.com

Library of Congress Cataloging-in-Publication Data
Jacobs, Daniel (Daniel Martin)
    City shapes / by Daniel Jacobs.
    p. cm.
    Summary: Simple text and photographs present common shapes that can be
found in buildings, signs, and other parts of a city.
    ISBN 0-7368-2915-6 (hardcover)—ISBN 0-7368-2874-5 (softcover)
    1. Shapes—Juvenile literature. [1. Shape. 2. Cities and towns.] I. Title.
QA445.5.J33 2004
516'.15—dc21   2003010972

Editorial Credits
Editorial Director: Mary Lindeen
Editor: Jennifer VanVoorst
Photo Researcher: Wanda Winch
Developer: Raindrop Publishing

Photo Credits
Cover: Jeffrey Greenberg/Index Stock Imagery; Title Page: Brett Patterson/Corbis;
Page 2: DigitalVision; Page 3: Jeffrey Greenberg/Folio, Inc.; Page 4: Robert C. Shafer/
Folio, Inc.; Page 5: PhotoLink/PhotoDisc; Page 6: Kent Knudson/PhotoLink/PhotoDisc;
Page 7: PhotoDisc/ Photodisc; Page 8: Robert C. Shafer/Folio, Inc.; Page 9: Ed
Castle/Folio, Inc.; Page 10: Image Farm; Page 11: C. Borland/PhotoLink/Photodisc;
Page 12: Kit Walling/Folio, Inc.; Page 13: Larry Brownstein/Photodisc; Page 14:
Richard Cummins/Corbis; Page 15: Reese Donovan/Photodisc; Page 16: Dallas and
John Heaton/Corbis

1 2 3 4 5 6 09 08 07 06 05 04

City Shapes

by Daniel Jacobs

Consultants: David Olson, Director of Undergraduate Studies, and Tamara Olson, PhD, Associate Professor, Department of Mathematical Studies, Michigan Technological University

Yellow Umbrella Books

an imprint of Capstone Press
Mankato, Minnesota

There is so much to see in a city!
There are tall buildings.

There are busy streets. What else can you see in a city?

You can see shapes! Do you see
the squares in this building?

4

There are squares in the
sidewalk, too!

Circles are city shapes, too. Do you see the circle in the street?

Whoosh! There are circles on this basketball court, too!

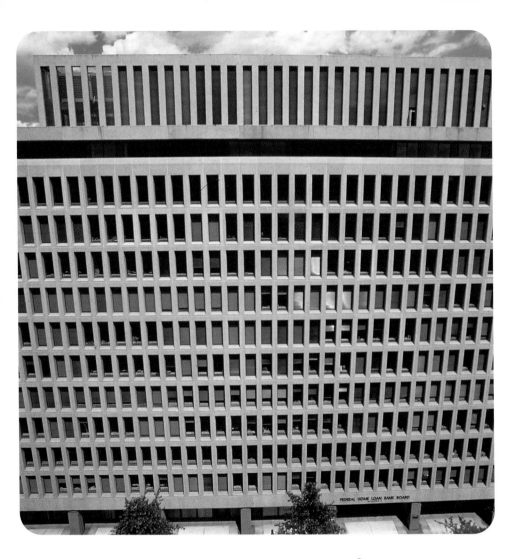

Rectangles are city shapes.
This building has too many
rectangles to count!

Look at the colorful doors.
These doors are rectangles, too.

Where can you see triangles in the city? Look at this sign!

Houses have shapes, too. Can you spot the triangles here?

Sometimes you can find different shapes in one place. What shapes do you see here?

Look at this bridge. Can you find the triangles and squares?

The sign for this city shop is a circle. The door is a rectangle.

The triangles on these boats help them sail. What shape are the buildings behind them?

A city is full of shapes! What kind of shape is this?

Words to Know/Index

basketball—a game played by two teams of five players each; players try to score points by throwing a ball through a high hoop at the end of the court; page 7

circle—a flat, perfectly round shape; pages 6, 7, 14

city—a very large town; pages 2, 3, 6, 8, 10, 14, 16

rectangle—a shape with four sides and four right angles; pages 8, 9, 14

shape—the form or outline of an object or a figure; pages 4, 6, 8, 11, 12, 15, 16

sidewalk—a paved path beside a street; page 5

square—a shape with four equal sides and four right angles; pages 4, 5, 13

triangle—a closed shape with three straight sides and three angles; pages 10, 11, 13, 15

Word Count: 177
Early-Intervention Level: 11